Song of Myself

SONG OF MYSELF

Walt Whitman

EDITED BY *Stephen Mitchell*

SHAMBHALA
Boston & London
1998

SHAMBHALA PUBLICATIONS, INC.
Horticultural Hall
300 Massachusetts Avenue
Boston, Massachusetts 02115
http://www.shambhala.com

This edition © 1993 by Stephen Mitchell

9   8   7   6   5   4   3   2   1

FIRST EDITION
Printed in the United States of America
⊗ This edition is printed on acid-free paper that meets the
American National Standards institute Z39.48 Standard.
Distributed in the United States by Random House, Inc.,
and in Canada by Random House of Canada Ltd

The Library of Congress catalogues the Shambhala Pocket
Classics edition of this book as follows:

Whitman, Walt, 1819–1892.
Song of myself/Walt Whitman;
edited by Stephen Mitchell.—1st Shambhala ed.
p.   cm.—(Shambhala pocket classics)
Includes bibliographical references (p.).
ISBN 0-87773-950-1 (Shambhala Pocket Classics)
ISBN 1-57062-369-4 (Shambhala Centaur Editions)
1. Whitman, Walt, 1819–1892.   Song of myself—
Criticism, Textual.   I. Mitchell, Stephen, 1943–
II. Title.   III. Series.
PS3222.S6   1993   93-20168
811.3—dc20   CIP

Contents

Editor's Preface

"Song of Myself" is by far the greatest poem ever written by an American. At each rereading I feel exhilarated, as if for the first time, by its freshness and breadth of vision, its bodiliness, its high spirits, its astonishing empathy, by the freedom and goofiness and dignity of its language, and, not least, by its spiritual insight. It is a miracle of a poem.

A few words about the text presented here. Whitman's vision and his language were at their most powerful in the first edition of *Leaves of Grass*, published in 1855. As he grew older, his insight faded, and with it the vivacity of his words. Yet in each successive edition he kept tinkering with "Song of Myself" and the other early poems—adding, deleting, revising. And while certain of these revisions are excellent, most of them are disastrous. This has led to an affectionate frustration among some of Whitman's readers; we want the best of all possible editions.

For example, in a passionate and deservedly famous passage about music the text of the 1855 edition reads:

> I hear the violincello or man's heart's complaint,
> And hear the keyed cornet or else the echo of
>   sunset.
>
> I hear the chorus . . . . it is a grand-opera . . . . this
>   indeed is music!
>
> A tenor large and fresh as the creation fills me,
> The orbic flex of his mouth is pouring and filling
>   me full.
>
> I hear the trained soprano . . . . she convulses me
>   like the climax of my love-grip;
> The orchestra whirls me wider than Uranus flies,
> It wrenches unnamable ardors from my breast,
> It throbs me to gulps of the farthest down horror,
> It sails me . . . . I dab with bare feet . . . . they are
>   licked by the indolent waves,
> I am exposed . . . . cut by bitter and poisoned
>   hail,
> Steeped amid honeyed morphine . . . . my
>   windpipe squeezed in the fakes
>   of death,
> Let up again to feel the puzzle of puzzles,
> And that we call Being.

Whitman incorporated two brilliant revisions in the second (1856) edition. There, line two reads:

> I hear the keyed cornet, it glides quickly in
>   through my ears, it shakes mad-sweet pangs
>   through my belly and breast.

And line eight:

> It wrenches such ardors from me, I did not know
>   I possessed them

In 1860 he rewrote the transition from lines twelve to thirteen in this way:

>   my windpipe throttled in fakes of
>   death,
> At length let up again to feel

On the other hand, in the 1867 and later editions Whitman ruined the sixth line by replacing its dangerous sexuality with a phrase that is colorless, almost meaningless, and a rhythm straight out of a hymn-book:

> I hear the trained soprano (what work with hers
>   is this?)

And he entirely deleted the weird and thrilling ninth line.

If I were forced to choose between the original and any of the revised versions, I would certainly choose the former. But why give up anything that makes a great poem even greater? Why not keep the revisions that enliven and clarify, and disregard the ones that don't? The passage then sounds like this:

> I hear the violincello or man's heart's complaint,
> I hear the keyed cornet, it glides quickly in
>   through my ears, it shakes mad-sweet pangs
>   through my belly and breast.
>
> I hear the chorus . . . . it is a grand-opera . . . . this
>   indeed is music!
>
> A tenor large and fresh as the creation fills me,
> The orbic flex of his mouth is pouring and filling
>   me full.
>
> I hear the trained soprano . . . . she convulses me
>   like the climax of my love-grip;
> The orchestra whirls me wider than Uranus flies,
> It wrenches such ardors from me, I did not know
>   I possessed them,
> It throbs me to gulps of the farthest down horror,

It sails me . . . . I dab with bare feet . . . . they are
    licked by the indolent waves,
I am exposed . . . . cut by bitter and poisoned
    hail,
Steeped amid honeyed morphine . . . . my
    windpipe throttled in fakes of death,
At length let up again to feel the puzzle of
    puzzles,
And that we call Being.

In this conflated version of "Song of Myself," I
have used the first edition as my main source, and I
have adopted any revision that seemed to be even a
minor improvement. The section numbers, which
first appeared in 1867, may be useful in providing a
more readily apparent structure, but they are often
arbitrary, and they impede the uninterrupted flow of
one stanza into the next, over the whole expanse of
the poem.

Although none of the poems had titles in the first
edition of *Leaves of Grass*, I have kept the 1876 edi-
tion's "Song of Myself" because it is so familiar.
Certainly the poem embodies an outrageous egotism,
an "I" so shamelessly naked that even a bodhisattva
can admire it. But Whitman was also writing about
selflessness, about the Self beyond the self ("I and

this mystery here we stand"; "Apart from the pulling and hauling stands what I am"), and it would have been just as appropriate to call the poem "Song of My Self," in the Upanishads' sense of the word:

Self is everywhere, shining forth from all beings,
vaster than the vast, subtler than the most subtle,
unreachable, yet nearer than breath, than heartbeat.

Egotism and selflessness: one contradiction among many. But the poem is large . . . . it contains and embraces multitudes.

SONG OF MYSELF

I celebrate myself,
And what I assume you shall assume,
For every atom belonging to me as good belongs to
     you.

I loafe and invite my soul,
I lean and loafe at my ease . . . . observing a spear of
     summer grass.

Houses and rooms are full of perfumes . . . . the
     shelves are crowded with perfumes,
I breathe the fragrance myself, and know it and like
     it,
The distillation would intoxicate me also, but I shall
     not let it.

The atmosphere is not a perfume . . . . it has no taste
     of the distillation . . . . it is odorless,
It is for my mouth forever . . . . I am in love with it,

I will go to the bank by the wood and become
    undisguised and naked,
I am mad for it to be in contact with me.

The smoke of my own breath,
Echoes, ripples, and buzzed whispers . . . . loveroot,
    silkthread, crotch and vine,
My respiration and inspiration . . . . the beating of
    my heart . . . . the passing of blood and air through
    my lungs,
The sniff of green leaves and dry leaves, and of the
    shore and darkcolored sea-rocks, and of hay in the
    barn,
The sound of the belched words of my voice
    . . . . words loosed to the eddies of the wind,
A few light kisses . . . . a few embraces . . . . a reaching
    around of arms,
The play of shine and shade on the trees as the
    supple boughs wag,
The delight alone or in the rush of the streets, or
    along the fields and hillsides,
The feeling of health . . . . the full-noon trill . . . . the
    song of me rising from bed and meeting the sun.

Have you reckoned a thousand acres much? Have
    you reckoned the earth much?

Have you practiced so long to learn to read?
Have you felt so proud to get at the meaning of
    poems?

Stop this day and night with me and you shall
    possess the origin of all poems,
You shall possess the good of the earth and sun
    . . . . there are millions of suns left,
You shall no longer take things at second or third
    hand . . . . nor look through the eyes of the dead
    . . . . nor feed on the spectres in books,
You shall not look through my eyes either, nor take
    things from me,
You shall listen to all sides and filter them from
    yourself.

I have heard what the talkers were talking . . . . the
    talk of the beginning and the end,
But I do not talk of the beginning or the end.

There was never any more inception than there is
    now,
Nor any more youth or age than there is now;
And will never be any more perfection than there is
    now,
Nor any more heaven or hell than there is now.

Urge and urge and urge,
Always the procreant urge of the world.

Out of the dimness opposite equals advance
    . . . . Always substance and increase, always sex,
Always a knit of identity . . . . always distinction
    . . . . always a breed of life.

To elaborate is no avail . . . . Learned and unlearned
    feel that it is so.

Sure as the most certain sure . . . . plumb in the
    uprights, well entretied, braced in the beams,
Stout as a horse, affectionate, haughty, electrical,
I and this mystery here we stand.

Clear and sweet is my soul . . . . and clear and sweet
    is all that is not my soul.

Lack one lacks both . . . . and the unseen is proved
    by the seen,
Till that becomes unseen and receives proof in its
    turn.

Showing the best and dividing it from the worst, age
    vexes age,

Knowing the perfect fitness and equanimity of
   things, while they discuss I am silent, and go bathe
   and admire myself.

Welcome is every organ and attribute of me, and of
   any man hearty and clean,
Not an inch nor a particle of an inch is vile, and
   none shall be less familiar than the rest.

I am satisfied . . . . I see, dance, laugh, sing;
As God comes a loving bedfellow and sleeps at my
   side all night and close on the peep of the day,
And leaves for me baskets covered with white towels
   bulging the house with their plenty,
Shall I postpone my acceptation and realization and
   scream at my eyes,
That they turn from gazing after and down the road,
And forthwith cipher and show me to a cent,
Exactly the contents of one, and exactly the contents
   of two, and which is ahead?

Trippers and askers surround me,
People I meet . . . . the effect upon me of my early
   life . . . . of the ward and city I live in . . . . of the
   nation,

The latest news . . . . discoveries, inventions, societies
. . . . authors old and new,
My dinner, dress, associates, looks, business,
compliments, dues,
The real or fancied indifference of some man or
woman I love,
The sickness of one of my folks—or of myself
. . . . or ill-doing . . . . or loss or lack of money
. . . . or depressions or exaltations,
They come to me days and nights and go from me
again,
But they are not the Me myself.

Apart from the pulling and hauling stands what I
am,
Stands amused, complacent, compassionating, idle,
unitary,
Looks down, is erect, bends an arm on an impalpable
certain rest,
Looks with its sidecurved head curious what will
come next,
Both in and out of the game, and watching and
wondering at it.

Backward I see in my own days where I sweated
through fog with linguists and contenders,

I have no mockings or arguments . . . . I witness and
    wait.

I believe in you my soul . . . . the other I am must
    not abase itself to you,
And you must not be abased to the other.

Loafe with me on the grass . . . . loose the stop from
    your throat,
Not words, not music or rhyme I want . . . . not
    custom or lecture, not even the best,
Only the lull I like, the hum of your valved voice.

I mind how we lay in June, such a transparent
    summer morning;
You settled your head athwart my hips and gently
    turned over upon me,
And parted the shirt from my bosom-bone, and
    plunged your tongue to my barestript heart,
And reached till you felt my beard, and reached till
    you held my feet.

Swiftly arose and spread around me the peace and
    knowledge that pass all the argument of the earth;
And I know that the hand of God is the elderhand
    of my own,

And I know that the spirit of God is the eldest
    brother of my own,
And that all the men ever born are also my brothers
    . . . . and the women my sisters and lovers,
And that a kelson of the creation is love;
And limitless are leaves stiff or drooping in the fields,
And brown ants in the little wells beneath them,
And mossy scabs of the wormfence, and heaped
    stones, and elder and mullen and pokeweed.

A child said, What is the grass? fetching it to me
    with full hands;
How could I answer the child? . . . . I do not know
    what it is any more than he.

I guess it must be the flag of my disposition, out of
    hopeful green stuff woven.

Or I guess it is the handkerchief of the Lord,
A scented gift and remembrancer designedly
    dropped,
Bearing the owner's name someway in the corners,
    that we may see and remark, and say Whose?

Or I guess the grass is itself a child . . . . the produced
    babe of the vegetation.

Or I guess it is a uniform hieroglyphic,
And it means, Sprouting alike in broad zones and
    narrow zones,
Growing among black folks as among white,
Kanuck, Tuckahoe, Congressman, Cuff, I give them
    the same, I receive them the same.

And now it seems to me the beautiful uncut hair of
    graves.

Tenderly will I use you curling grass,
It may be you transpire from the breasts of young
    men,
It may be if I had known them I would have loved
    them;
It may be you are from old people, or from offspring
    taken soon out of their mothers' laps,
And here you are the mothers' laps.

This grass is very dark to be from the white heads of
    old mothers,
Darker than the colorless beards of old men,
Dark to come from under the faint red roofs of
    mouths.

O I perceive after all so many uttering tongues!
And I perceive they do not come from the roofs of
    mouths for nothing.

I wish I could translate the hints about the dead
    young men and women,
And the hints about old men and mothers, and the
    offspring taken soon out of their laps.

What do you think has become of the young and
    old men?
And what do you think has become of the women
    and children?

They are alive and well somewhere;
The smallest sprout shows there is really no death,
And if ever there was it led forward life, and does
    not wait at the end to arrest it,
And ceased the moment life appeared.

All goes onward and outward . . . . and nothing
    collapses,
And to die is different from what any one supposed,
    and luckier.

Has any one supposed it lucky to be born?
I hasten to inform him or her it is just as lucky to
    die, and I know it.

I pass death with the dying, and birth with the new-
    washed babe . . . . and am not contained between
    my hat and boots,
And peruse manifold objects, no two alike, and every
    one good,
The earth good, and the stars good, and their
    adjuncts all good.

I am not an earth nor an adjunct of an earth,
I am the mate and companion of people, all just as
    immortal and fathomless as myself;
They do not know how immortal, but I know.

Every kind for itself and its own . . . . for me mine
    male and female,
For me all that have been boys and that love women,
For me the man that is proud and feels how it stings
    to be slighted,
For me the sweetheart and the old maid . . . . for me
    mothers and the mothers of mothers,
For me lips that have smiled, eyes that have shed
    tears,
For me children and the begetters of children.

Who need be afraid of the merge?
Undrape . . . . you are not guilty to me, nor stale nor
    discarded,

I see through the broadcloth and gingham whether
    or no,
And am around, tenacious, acquisitive, tireless
    . . . . and can never be shaken away.

The little one sleeps in its cradle,
I lift the gauze and look a long time, and silently
    brush away flies with my hand.

The youngster and the redfaced girl turn aside up
    the bushy hill,
I peeringly view them from the top.

The suicide sprawls on the bloody floor of the
    bedroom,
I witness the corpse with its dabbled hair, I note
    where the pistol has fallen.

The blab of the pave . . . . the tires of carts and sluff
    of bootsoles and talk of the promenaders,
The heavy omnibus, the driver with his interrogating
    thumb, the clank of the shod horses on the granite
    floor,
The carnival of sleighs, the clinking and shouted
    jokes and pelts of snowballs;

The hurrahs for popular favorites . . . . the fury of
   roused mobs,
The flap of the curtained litter—the sick man inside,
   borne to the hospital,
The meeting of enemies, the sudden oath, the blows
   and fall,
The excited crowd—the policeman with his star
   quickly working his passage to the centre of the
   crowd;
The impassive stones that receive and return so many
   echoes,
The souls moving along . . . . are they invisible while
   the least atom of the stones is visible?
What groans of overfed or half-starved who fall on
   the flags sunstruck or in fits,
What exclamations of women taken suddenly, who
   hurry home and give birth to babes,
What living and buried speech is always vibrating
   here . . . . what howls restrained by decorum,
Arrests of criminals, slights, adulterous offers made,
   acceptances, rejections with convex lips,
I mind them or the resonance of them . . . . I come
   and I depart.

The big doors of the country-barn stand open and
   ready,

The dried grass of the harvest-time loads the slow-
    drawn wagon,
The clear light plays on the brown gray and green
    intertinged,
The armfuls are packed to the sagging mow:
I am there . . . . I help . . . . I came stretched atop of
    the load,
I felt its soft jolts . . . . one leg reclined on the other,
I jump from the crossbeams, and seize the clover and
    timothy,
And roll head over heels, and tangle my hair full of
    wisps.

Alone far in the wilds and mountains I hunt,
Wandering amazed at my own lightness and glee,
In the late afternoon choosing a safe spot to pass the
    night,
Kindling a fire and broiling the freshkilled game,
Falling asleep on the gathered leaves, my dog and
    gun by my side.

The Yankee clipper is under her three skysails
    . . . . she cuts the sparkle and scud,
My eyes settle the land . . . . I bend at her prow or
    shout joyously from the deck.

The boatmen and clamdiggers arose early and
   stopped for me,
I tucked my trowser-ends in my boots and went and
   had a good time,
You should have been with us that day round the
   chowder-kettle.

I saw the marriage of the trapper in the open air in
   the far-west . . . . the bride was a red girl,
Her father and his friends sat near by crosslegged
   and dumbly smoking . . . . they had moccasins to
   their feet and large thick blankets hanging from
   their shoulders;
On a bank lounged the trapper . . . . he was dressed
   mostly in skins . . . . his luxuriant beard and curls
   protected his neck. . . . he held his bride by the
   hand,
She had long eyelashes . . . . her head was bare
   . . . . her coarse straight locks descended upon her
   voluptuous limbs and reached to her feet.

The runaway slave came to my house and stopped
   outside,
I heard his motions crackling the twigs of the
   woodpile,

Through the swung half-door of the kitchen I saw
    him limpsy and weak,
And went where he sat on a log, and led him in and
    assured him,
And brought water and filled a tub for his sweated
    body and bruised feet,
And gave him a room that entered from my own,
    and gave him some coarse clean clothes,
And remember perfectly well his revolving eyes and
    his awkwardness,
And remember putting plasters on the galls of his
    neck and ankles;
He staid with me a week before he was recuperated
    and passed north,
I had him sit next me at table . . . . my firelock leaned
    in the corner.

Twenty-eight young men bathe by the shore,
Twenty-eight young men, and all so friendly,
Twenty-eight years of womanly life, and all so
    lonesome.

She owns the fine house by the rise of the bank,
She hides handsome and richly drest aft the blinds
    of the window.

Which of the young men does she like the best?
Ah the homeliest of them is beautiful to her.

Where are you off to, lady? for I see you,
You splash in the water there, yet stay stock still in
    your room.

Dancing and laughing along the beach came the
    twenty-ninth bather,
The rest did not see her, but she saw them and loved
    them.

The beards of the young men glistened with wet, it
    ran from their long hair,
Little streams passed all over their bodies.

An unseen hand also passed over their bodies,
It descended tremblingly from their temples and ribs.

The young men float on their backs, their white
    bellies swell to the sun . . . . they do not ask who
    seizes fast to them,
They do not know who puffs and declines with
    pendant and bending arch,
They do not think whom they souse with spray.

The butcher-boy puts off his killing-clothes, or
  sharpens his knife at the stall in the market,
I loiter enjoying his repartee and his shuffle and
  breakdown.

Blacksmiths with grimed and hairy chests environ the
  anvil,
Each has his main-sledge . . . . they are all out
  . . . . there is a great heat in the fire.

From the cinder-strewed threshold I follow their
  movements,
The lithe sheer of their waists plays even with their
  massive arms,
Overhand the hammers roll—overhand so
  slow—overhand so sure,
They do not hasten, each man hits in his place.

The negro holds firmly the reins of his four horses
  . . . . the block swags underneath on its tied-over
  chain,
The negro that drives the huge dray of the stoneyard
  . . . . steady and tall he stands poised on one leg
  on the stringpiece,
His blue shirt exposes his ample neck and breast and
  loosens over his hipband,

His glance is calm and commanding . . . . he tosses
    the slouch of his hat away from his forehead,
The sun falls on his crispy hair and moustache
    . . . . falls on the black of his polish'd and perfect
    limbs.

I behold the picturesque giant and love him . . . . and
    I do not stop there,
I go with the team also.

In me the caresser of life wherever moving
    . . . . backward as well as forward slueing,
To niches aside and junior bending.

Oxen that rattle the yoke or halt in the shade, what
    is that you express in your eyes?
It seems to me more than all the print I have read in
    my life.

My tread scares the wood-drake and wood-duck on
    my distant and daylong ramble,
They rise together, they slowly circle around.
. . . . I believe in those winged purposes,
And acknowledge the red yellow and white playing
    within me,

And consider the green and violet and the tufted
    crown intentional;
And do not call the tortoise unworthy because she is
    not something else,
And the mockingbird in the swamp never studied the
    gamut, yet trills pretty well to me,
And the look of the bay mare shames silliness out of
    me.

The wild gander leads his flock through the cool
    night,
Ya-honk! he says, and sounds it down to me like an
    invitation;
The pert may suppose it meaningless, but I listen
    closer,
I find its purpose and place up there toward the
    November sky.

The sharphoofed moose of the north, the cat on the
    housesill, the chickadee, the prairie-dog,
The litter of the grunting sow as they tug at her teats,
The brood of the turkeyhen, and she with her
    halfspread wings,
I see in them and myself the same old law.

The press of my foot to the earth springs a hundred
    affections,
They scorn the best I can do to relate them.

I am enamoured of growing outdoors,
Of men that live among cattle or taste of the ocean
    or woods,
Of the builders and steerers of ships, of the wielders
    of axes and mauls, of the drivers of horses,
I can eat and sleep with them week in and week out.

What is commonest and cheapest and nearest and
    easiest is Me,
Me going in for my chances, spending for vast
    returns,
Adorning myself to bestow myself on the first that
    will take me,
Not asking the sky to come down to my goodwill,
Scattering it freely forever.

The pure contralto sings in the organloft,
The carpenter dresses his plank . . . . the tongue of
    his foreplane whistles its wild ascending lisp,
The married and unmarried children ride home to
    their Thanksgiving dinner,

The pilot seizes the king-pin, he heaves down with a
    strong arm,
The mate stands braced in the whaleboat, lance and
    harpoon are ready,
The duck-shooter walks by silent and cautious
    stretches,
The deacons are ordained with crossed hands at the
    altar,
The spinning-girl retreats and advances to the hum
    of the big wheel,
The farmer stops by the bars of a Sunday and looks
    at the oats and rye,
The lunatic is carried at last to the asylum a
    confirmed case,
He will never sleep any more as he did in the cot in
    his mother's bedroom;
The jour printer with gray head and gaunt jaws
    works at his case,
He turns his quid of tobacco, his eyes get blurred
    with the manuscript;
The malformed limbs are tied to the anatomist's
    table,
What is removed drops horribly in a pail;
The quadroon girl is sold at the auction-stand
    . . . . the drunkard nods by the barroom stove,

The machinist rolls up his sleeves . . . . the policeman
    travels his beat . . . . the gate-keeper marks who pass,
The young fellow drives the express-wagon . . . .
    I love him though I do not know him;
The half-breed straps on his light boots to compete
    in the race,
The western turkey-shooting draws old and young
    . . . . some lean on their rifles, some sit on logs,
Out from the crowd steps the marksman and takes
    his position and levels his piece;
The groups of newly-come immigrants cover the
    wharf or levee,
The woollypates hoe in the sugarfield, the overseer
    views them from his saddle;
The bugle calls in the ballroom, the gentlemen run
    for their partners, the dancers bow to each other;
The youth lies awake in the cedar-roofed garret and
    harks to the musical rain,
The Wolverine sets traps on the creek that helps fill
    the Huron,
The reformer ascends the platform, he spouts with
    his mouth and nose,
The company returns from its excursion, the darkey
    brings up the rear and bears the well-riddled
    target,

The squaw wrapt in her yellow-hemmed cloth is
    offering moccasins and beadbags for sale,
The connoisseur peers along the exhibition-gallery
    with halfshut eyes bent sideways,
The deckhands make fast the steamboat, the plank
    is thrown for the shoregoing passengers,
The young sister holds out the skein, the elder sister
    winds it off in a ball and stops now and then for
    the knots,
The one-year wife is recovering and happy, a week
    ago she bore her first child,
The cleanhaired Yankee girl works with her sewing-
    machine or in the factory or mill,
The nine months' gone is in the parturition chamber,
    her faintness and pains are advancing;
The pavingman leans on his twohanded
    rammer—the reporter's lead flies swiftly over the
    notebook—the signpainter is lettering with red
    and gold,
The canal-boy trots on the towpath—the
    bookkeeper counts at his desk—the shoemaker
    waxes his thread,
The conductor beats time for the band and all the
    performers follow him,
The child is baptised—the convert is making his first
    professions,

The regatta is spread on the bay . . . . how the white
    sails sparkle!
The drover watches his drove, he sings out to them
    that would stray,
The pedlar sweats with his pack on his back——the
    purchaser higgles about the odd cent,
The camera and plate are prepared, the lady must sit
    for her daguerreotype,
The bride unrumples her white dress, the
    minutehand of the clock moves slowly,
The opium eater reclines with rigid head and just-
    opened lips,
The prostitute draggles her shawl, her bonnet bobs
    on her tipsy and pimpled neck,
The crowd laugh at her blackguard oaths, the men
    jeer and wink to each other,
(Miserable! I do not laugh at your oaths nor jeer
    you,)
The President holds a cabinet council, he is
    surrounded by the great secretaries,
On the piazza walk five friendly matrons with twined
    arms;
The crew of the fish-smack pack repeated layers of
    halibut in the hold,
The Missourian crosses the plains toting his wares
    and his cattle,

The fare-collector goes through the train—he gives
    notice by the jingling of loose change,
The floormen are laying the floor—the tinners are
    tinning the roof—the masons are calling for
    mortar,
In single file each shouldering his hod pass onward
    the laborers;
Seasons pursuing each other the indescribable crowd
    is gathered . . . . it is the Fourth of July . . . . what
    salutes of cannon and small arms!
Seasons pursuing each other the plougher ploughs
    and the mower mows and the wintergrain falls in
    the ground;
Off on the lakes the pikefisher watches and waits by
    the hole in the frozen surface,
The stumps stand thick round the clearing, the
    squatter strikes deep with his axe,
The flatboatmen make fast toward dusk near the
    cottonwood or pekantrees,
The coon-seekers go now through the regions of the
    Red river, or through those drained by the
    Tennessee, or through those of the Arkansas,
The torches shine in the dark that hangs on the
    Chattahoochee or Altamahaw;
Patriarchs sit at supper with sons and grandsons and
    great grandsons around them,

In walls of adobe, in canvas tents, rest hunters and
    trappers after their day's sport.
The city sleeps and the country sleeps,
The living sleep for their time . . . . the dead sleep
    for their time,
The old husband sleeps by his wife and the young
    husband sleeps by his wife;
And these one and all tend inward to me, and I tend
    outward to them,
And such as it is to be of these more or less I am.

I am of old and young, of the foolish as much as the
    wise,
Regardless of others, ever regardful of others,
Maternal as well as paternal, a child as well as a man,
Stuffed with the stuff that is coarse, and stuffed with
    the stuff that is fine,
One of the great nation, the nation of many
    nations—the smallest the same and the largest the
    same,
A southerner soon as a northerner, a planter
    nonchalant and hospitable,
A Yankee bound my own way . . . . ready for trade
    . . . . my joints the limberest joints on earth and
    the sternest joints on earth,

A Kentuckian walking the vale of the Elkhorn in my
   deerskin leggings,
A boatman over the lakes or bays or along coasts
   . . . . a Hoosier, a Badger, a Buckeye,
A Louisianian or Georgian, a poke-easy from
   sandhills and pines,
At home on Canadian snowshoes or up in the bush,
   or with fishermen off Newfoundland,
At home in the fleet of iceboats, sailing with the rest
   and tacking,
At home on the hills of Vermont or in the woods of
   Maine or the Texan ranch,
Comrade of Californians . . . . comrade of free
   northwesterners, loving their big proportions,
Comrade of raftsmen and coalmen—comrade of all
   who shake hands and welcome to drink and meat;
A learner with the simplest, a teacher of the
   thoughtfulest,
A novice beginning experient of myriads of seasons,
Of every hue and trade and rank, of every caste and
   religion,
Not merely of the New World but of Africa Europe
   or Asia . . . . a wandering savage,
A farmer, mechanic, or artist . . . . a gentleman, sailor,
   lover or quaker,
A prisoner, fancy-man, rowdy, lawyer, physician or
   priest.

I resist anything better than my own diversity,
And breathe the air and leave plenty after me,
And am not stuck up, and am in my place.

The moth and the fisheggs are in their place,
The suns I see and the suns I cannot see are in their
place,
The palpable is in its place and the impalpable is in
its place.

These are the thoughts of all men in all ages and
lands, they are not original with me,
If they are not yours as much as mine they are
nothing or next to nothing,
If they do not enclose everything they are next to
nothing,
If they are not the riddle and the untying of the
riddle they are nothing,
If they are not just as close as they are distant they
are nothing.

This is the grass that grows wherever the land is and
the water is,
This is the common air that bathes the globe.

This is the breath of laws and songs and behavior,
This is the tasteless water of souls . . . . this is the
true sustenance,

It is for the illiterate . . . . it is for the judges of the
supreme court . . . . it is for the federal capitol and
the state capitols,
It is for the admirable communes of literary men and
composers and singers and lecturers and engineers
and savans,
It is for the endless races of working people and
farmers and seamen.

This is the trill of a thousand clear cornets and
scream of the octave flute and strike of triangles.

I play not a march for victors only . . . . I play great
marches for conquered and slain persons.

Have you heard that it was good to gain the day?
I also say it is good to fall . . . . battles are lost in the
same spirit in which they are won.

I sound triumphal drums for the dead . . . . I fling
through my embouchures the loudest and gayest
music to them,
Vivas to those who have failed, and to those whose
war-vessels sank in the sea, and those themselves
who sank in the sea,
And to all generals that lost engagements, and all

overcome heroes, and the numberless unknown
   heroes equal to the greatest heroes known.

This is the meal pleasantly set . . . . this is the meat
   and drink for natural hunger,
It is for the wicked just the same as the righteous
   . . . . I make appointments with all,
I will not have a single person slighted or left away,
The keptwoman and sponger and thief are hereby
   invited . . . . the heavy-lipped slave is invited
   . . . . the venerealee is invited,
There shall be no difference between them and the
   rest.

This is the press of a bashful hand . . . . this is the
   float and odor of hair,
This is the touch of my lips to yours . . . . this is the
   murmur of yearning,
This is the far-off depth and height reflecting my
   own face,
This is the thoughtful merge of myself and the outlet
   again.

Do you guess I have some intricate purpose?
Well I have . . . . for the April rain has, and the mica
   on the side of a rock has.

Do you take it I would astonish?
Does the daylight astonish? or the early redstart
    twittering through the woods?
Do I astonish more than they?

This hour I tell things in confidence,
I might not tell everybody but I will tell you.

Who goes there! hankering, gross, mystical, nude?
How is it I extract strength from the beef I eat?

What is a man anyhow? What am I? and what are
    you?
All I mark as my own you shall offset it with your
    own,
Else it were time lost listening to me.

I do not snivel that snivel the world over,
That months are vacuums and the ground but
    wallow and filth,
That life is a suck and a sell, and nothing remains at
    the end but threadbare crape and tears.

Whimpering and truckling fold with powders for
    invalids . . . . conformity goes to the fourth-
    removed,
I cock my hat as I please indoors or out.

Why should I pray? Why should I venerate and be
    ceremonious?

Having pried through the strata and analyzed to a
    hair, and counselled with doctors and calculated
    close,
I find no sweeter fat than sticks to my own bones.

In all people I see myself, none more and not one a
    barleycorn less,
And the good or bad I say of myself I say of them.

And I know I am solid and sound,
To me the converging objects of the universe
    perpetually flow,
All are written to me, and I must get what the writing
    means.

And I know I am deathless,
I know this orbit of mine cannot be swept by a
    carpenter's compass,
I know I shall not pass like a child's carlacue cut
    with a burnt stick at night.

I know I am august,
I do not trouble my spirit to vindicate itself or be
    understood,

I see that the elementary laws never apologize,
I reckon I behave no prouder than the level I plant
    my house by after all.

I exist as I am, that is enough,
If no other in the world be aware I sit content,
And if each and all be aware I sit content.

One world is aware, and by far the largest to me, and
    that is myself,
And whether I come to my own today or in ten
    thousand or ten million years,
I can cheerfully take it now, or with equal
    cheerfulness I can wait.

My foothold is tenoned and mortised in granite,
I laugh at what you call dissolution,
And I know the amplitude of time.

I am the poet of the body,
And I am the poet of the soul.

The pleasures of heaven are with me, and the pains
    of hell are with me,
The first I graft and increase upon myself . . . . the
    latter I translate into a new tongue.

I am the poet of the woman the same as the man,
And I say it is as great to be a woman as to be a
   man,
And I say there is nothing greater than the mother
   of men.

I chant a new chant of dilation or pride,
We have had ducking and deprecating about enough,
I show that size is only development.

Have you outstript the rest? Are you the President?
It is a trifle . . . . they will more than arrive there
   every one, and still pass on.

I am he that walks with the tender and growing
   night;
I call to the earth and sea half-held by the night.
Press close barebosomed night! Press close magnetic
   nourishing night!
Night of south winds! Night of the large few stars!
Still nodding night! Mad naked summer night!

Smile O voluptuous coolbreathed earth!
Earth of the slumbering and liquid trees!
Earth of departed sunset! Earth of the mountains
   misty-topt!

Earth of the vitreous pour of the full moon just
    tinged with blue!
Earth of shine and dark mottling the tide of the river!
Earth of the limpid gray of clouds brighter and
    clearer for my sake!
Far-swooping elbowed earth! Rich apple-blossomed
    earth!
Smile, for your lover comes!

Prodigal! you have given me love! .... therefore I to
    you give love!
O unspeakable passionate love!

Thruster holding me tight and that I hold tight!
We hurt each other as the bridegroom and the bride
    hurt each other.

You sea! I resign myself to you also .... I guess what
    you mean,
I behold from the beach your crooked inviting
    fingers,
I believe you refuse to go back without feeling of
    me;
We must have a turn together .... I undress
    .... hurry me out of sight of the land,

Cushion me soft . . . . rock me in billowy drowse,
Dash me with amorous wet . . . . I can repay you.

Sea of stretched ground-swells!
Sea breathing broad and convulsive breaths!
Sea of the brine of life! Sea of unshovelled and
    always-ready graves!
Howler and scooper of storms! Capricious and
    dainty sea!
I am integral with you . . . . I too am of one phase
    and of all phases.

Partaker of influx and efflux . . . . extoler of hate and
    conciliation,
Extoler of amies and those that sleep in each others'
    arms.

I am he attesting sympathy;
Shall I make my list of things in the house and skip
    the house that supports them?

I am the poet of commonsense and of the
    demonstrable and of immortality;
And am not the poet of goodness only . . . . I do not
    decline to be the poet of wickedness also.

Washes and razors for foofoos . . . . for me freckles
    and a bristling beard.

What blurt is it about virtue and about vice?
Evil propels me, and reform of evil propels me . . . .
    I stand indifferent,
My gait is no faultfinder's or rejecter's gait,
I moisten the roots of all that has grown.

Did you fear some scrofula out of the unflagging
    pregnancy?
Did you guess the celestial laws are yet to be worked
    over and rectified?

I step up to say that what we do is right and what
    we affirm is right . . . . and some is only the ore
    of right,
Witnesses of us . . . . one side a balance and the
    antipodal side a balance,
Soft doctrine as steady help as stable doctrine,
Thoughts and deeds of the present our rouse and
    early start.

This minute that comes to me over the past
    decillions,
There is no better than it and now.

What behaved well in the past or behaves well today
  is not such a wonder,
The wonder is always and always how there can be a
  mean man or an infidel.

Endless unfolding of words of ages!
And mine a word of the modern . . . . a word en
  masse.

A word of the faith that never balks,
One time as good as another time . . . . here or
  henceforward it is all the same to me.

A word of reality . . . . materialism first and last
  imbuing.

Hurrah for positive science! Long live exact
  demonstration!
Fetch stonecrop and mix it with cedar and branches
  of lilac;
This is the lexicographer or chemist . . . . this made
  a grammar of the old cartouches,
These mariners put the ship through dangerous
  unknown seas,
This is the geologist, and this works with the scalpel,
  and this is a mathematician.

Gentlemen I receive you, and attach and clasp hands
    with you,
The facts are useful and real . . . . they are not my
    dwelling . . . . I enter by them to an area of the
    dwelling.

I am less the reminder of property or qualities, and
    more the reminder of life,
And go on the square for my own sake and for
    others' sakes,
And make short account of neuters and geldings, and
    favor men and women fully equipped,
And beat the gong of revolt, and stop with fugitives
    and them that plot and conspire.

Walt Whitman, an American, one of the roughs, a
    kosmos,
Disorderly fleshy and sensual . . . . eating drinking
    and breeding,
No sentimentalist . . . . no stander above men and
    women or apart from them . . . . no more modest
    than immodest.

Unscrew the locks from the doors!
Unscrew the doors themselves from their jambs!

Whoever degrades another degrades me . . . . and
    whatever is done or said returns at last to me,
And whatever I do or say I also return.

Through me the afflatus surging and surging
    . . . . through me the current and index.

I speak the password primeval . . . . I give the sign of
    democracy;
By God! I will accept nothing which all cannot have
    their counterpart of on the same terms.

Through me many long dumb voices,
Voices of the interminable generations of slaves,
Voices of prostitutes and of deformed persons,
Voices of the diseased and despairing, and of thieves
    and dwarfs,
Voices of cycles of preparation and accretion,
And of the threads that connect the stars—and of
    wombs, and of the fatherstuff,
And of the rights of them the others are down upon,
Of the trivial and flat and foolish and despised,
Of fog in the air and beetles rolling balls of dung.

Through me forbidden voices,
Voices of sexes and lusts . . . . voices veiled, and I
    remove the veil,
Voices indecent by me clarified and transfigured.

I do not press my finger across my mouth,
I keep as delicate around the bowels as around the
    head and heart,
Copulation is no more rank to me than death is.

I believe in the flesh and the appetites,
Seeing hearing and feeling are miracles, and each part
    and tag of me is a miracle.

Divine am I inside and out, and I make holy
    whatever I touch or am touched from;
The scent of these arm-pits is aroma finer than
    prayer,
This head is more than churches or bibles or creeds.

If I worship one thing more than another it shall be
    the spread of my own body, or any part of it;
Translucent mould of me it shall be you,
Shaded ledges and rests, firm masculine coulter, it
    shall be you,
Whatever goes to the tilth of me it shall be you,
You my rich blood, your milky stream pale
    strippings of my life;
Breast that presses against other breasts it shall be
    you,
My brain it shall be your occult convolutions,
Root of washed sweet-flag, timorous pond-snipe,
    nest of guarded duplicate eggs, it shall be you,
Mixed tussled hay of head and beard and brawn it
    shall be you,

Trickling sap of maple, fibre of manly wheat, it shall
    be you;
Sun so generous it shall be you,
Vapors lighting and shading my face it shall be you,
You sweaty brooks and dews it shall be you,
Winds whose soft-tickling genitals rub against me it
    shall be you,
Broad muscular fields, branches of liveoak, loving
    lounger in my winding paths, it shall be you,
Hands I have taken, face I have kissed, mortal I have
    ever touched, it shall be you.

I dote on myself . . . . there is that lot of me, and all
    so luscious,
Each moment and whatever happens thrills me with
    joy.

I cannot tell how my ankles bend . . . . nor whence
    the cause of my faintest wish,
Nor the cause of the friendship I emit . . . . nor the
    cause of the friendship I take again.

To walk up my stoop is unaccountable . . . . I pause
    to consider if it really be,
That I eat and drink is spectacle enough for the great
    authors and schools,

A morning-glory at my window satisfies me more
  than the metaphysics of books.

To behold the daybreak!
The little light fades the immense and diaphanous
  shadows,
The air tastes good to my palate.

Hefts of the moving world at innocent gambols,
  silently rising, freshly exuding,
Scooting obliquely high and low.

Something I cannot see puts upward libidinous
  prongs,
Seas of bright juice suffuse heaven.

The earth by the sky staid with . . . . the daily close
  of their junction,
The heaved challenge from the east that moment
  over my head,
The mocking taunt, See then whether you shall be
  master!

Dazzling and tremendous how quick the sunrise
  would kill me,

If I could not now and always send sunrise out of
   me.

We also ascend dazzling and tremendous as the sun,
We found our own my soul in the calm and cool of
   the daybreak.

My voice goes after what my eyes cannot reach,
With the twirl of my tongue I encompass worlds
   and volumes of worlds.

Speech is the twin of my vision . . . . it is unequal to
   measure itself.

It provokes me forever,
It says sarcastically, Walt, you understand enough
   . . . . why don't you let it out then?

Come now I will not be tantalized . . . . you conceive
   too much of articulation.

Do you not know how the buds beneath are folded?
Waiting in gloom protected by frost,
The dirt receding before my prophetical screams,
I underlying causes to balance them at last,

My knowledge my live parts . . . . it keeping tally
    with the meaning of things,
Happiness . . . . which whoever hears me let him or
    her set out in search of this day.

My final merit I refuse you . . . . I refuse putting
    from me the best I am.

Encompass worlds but never try to encompass me,
I crowd your noisiest talk by looking toward you.

Writing and talk do not prove me,
I carry the plenum of proof and every thing else in
    my face,
With the hush of my lips I confound the topmost
    skeptic.

I think I will do nothing for a long time but listen,
And accrue what I hear into myself . . . . and let
    sounds contribute toward me.

I hear the bravuras of birds . . . . the bustle of
    growing wheat . . . . gossip of flames . . . . clack of
    sticks cooking my meals.

I hear the sound of the human voice . . . . a sound I
    love,

I hear all sounds as they are tuned to their uses
  . . . . sounds of the city and sounds out of the city
  . . . . sounds of the day and night;
Talkative young ones to those that like them . . . . the
  recitative of fish-pedlars and fruit-pedlars . . . . the
  loud laugh of workpeople at their meals,
The angry base of disjointed friendship . . . . the
  faint tones of the sick,
The judge with hands tight to the desk, his shaky
  lips pronouncing a death-sentence,
The heave'e'yo of stevedores unlading ships by the
  wharves . . . . the refrain of the anchor-lifters;
The ring of alarm-bells . . . . the cry of fire . . . . the
  whirr of swift-streaking engines and hose-carts
  with premonitory tinkles and colored lights,
The steam-whistle . . . . the solid roll of the train of
  approaching cars;
The slow-march played at night at the head of the
  association,
They go to guard some corpse . . . . the flag-tops are
  draped with black muslin.

I hear the violoncello or man's heart's complaint,
I hear the keyed cornet, it glides quickly in through
  my ears, it shakes mad-sweet pangs through my
  belly and breast.

I hear the chorus . . . . it is a grand-opera . . . . this
     indeed is music!

A tenor large and fresh as the creation fills me,
The orbic flex of his mouth is pouring and filling me
     full.

I hear the trained soprano . . . . she convulses me like
     the climax of my love-grip;
The orchestra whirls me wider than Uranus flies,
It wrenches such ardors from me, I did not know I
     possessed them,
It throbs me to gulps of the farthest down horror,
It sails me . . . . I dab with bare feet . . . . they are
     licked by the indolent waves,
I am exposed . . . . cut by bitter and poisoned hail,
Steeped amid honeyed morphine . . . . my windpipe
     throttled in fakes of death,
At length let up again to feel the puzzle of puzzles,
And that we call Being.

To be in any form, what is that?
If nothing lay more developed the quahaug and its
     callous shell were enough.

Mine is no callous shell,
I have instant conductors all over me whether I pass
    or stop,
They seize every object and lead it harmlessly
    through me.

I merely stir, press, feel with my fingers, and am
    happy,
To touch my person to some one else's is about as
    much as I can stand.

Is this then a touch? . . . . quivering me to a new
    identity,
Flames and ether making a rush for my veins,
Treacherous tip of me reaching and crowding to help
    them,
My flesh and blood playing out lightning, to strike
    what is hardly different from myself,
On all sides prurient provokers stiffening my limbs,
Straining the udder of my heart for its withheld drip,
Behaving licentious toward me, taking no denial,
Depriving me of my best as for a purpose,
Unbuttoning my clothes and holding me by the bare
    waist,

Deluding my confusion with the calm of the sunlight
and pasture fields,
Immodestly sliding the fellow-senses away,
They bribed to swap off with touch, and go and
graze at the edges of me,
No consideration, no regard for my draining
strength or my anger,
Fetching the rest of the herd around to enjoy them
awhile,
Then all uniting to stand on a headland and worry
me.

The sentries desert every other part of me,
They have left me helpless to a red marauder,
They all come to the headland to witness and assist
against me.

I am given up by traitors;
I talk wildly . . . . I have lost my wits . . . . I and
nobody else am the greatest traitor,
I went myself first to the headland . . . . my own
hands carried me there.

You villain touch! what are you doing? . . . . my
breath is tight in its throat;
Unclench your floodgates! you are too much for me.

Blind loving wrestling touch! Sheathed hooded
  sharptoothed touch!
Did it make you ache so leaving me?

Parting tracked by arriving . . . . perpetual payment
  of the perpetual loan,
Rich showering rain, and recompense richer
  afterward.

Sprouts take and accumulate . . . . stand by the curb
  prolific and vital,
Landscapes projected masculine full-sized and
  golden.

All truths wait in all things,
They neither hasten their own delivery nor resist it,
They do not need the obstetric forceps of the
  surgeon,
The insignificant is as big to me as any,
What is less or more than a touch?

Logic and sermons never convince,
The damp of the night drives deeper into my soul.

Only what proves itself to every man and woman is
  so,
Only what nobody denies is so.

A minute and a drop of me settle my brain;
I believe the soggy clods shall become lovers and
    lamps,
And a compend of compends is the meat of a man
    or woman,
And a summit and flower there is the feeling they
    have for each other,
And they are to branch boundlessly out of that
    lesson until it becomes omnific,
And until every one shall delight us, and we them.

I believe a leaf of grass is no less than the
    journeywork of the stars,
And the pismire is equally perfect, and a grain of
    sand, and the egg of the wren,
And the tree-toad is a chef-d'œuvre for the highest,
And the running blackberry would adorn the parlors
    of heaven,
And the narrowest hinge in my hands puts to scorn
    all machinery,
And the cow crunching with depressed head
    surpasses any statue,
And a mouse is miracle enough to stagger sextillions
    of infidels.

I find I incorporate gneiss and coal and long-
    threaded moss and fruits and grains and esculent
    roots,
And am stucco'd with quadrupeds and birds all over,
And have distanced what is behind me for good
    reasons,
And call any thing close again when I desire it.

In vain the speeding or shyness,
In vain the plutonic rocks send their old heat against
    my approach,
In vain the mastodon retreats beneath its own
    powdered bones,
In vain objects stand leagues off and assume
    manifold shapes,
In vain the ocean settling in hollows and the great
    monsters lying low,
In vain the buzzard houses herself with the sky,
In vain the snake slides through the creepers and
    logs,
In vain the elk takes to the inner passes of the woods,
In vain the razorbilled auk sails far north to
    Labrador,
I follow quickly . . . . I ascend to the nest in the
    fissure of the cliff.

I think I could turn and live awhile with the animals
    . . . . they are so placid and self-contained,
I stand and look at them long and long.

They do not sweat and whine about their condition,
They do not lie awake in the dark and weep for their
    sins,
They do not make me sick discussing their duty to
    God,
Not one is dissatisfied . . . . not one is demented with
    the mania of owning things,
Not one kneels to another nor to his kind that lived
    thousands of years ago,
Not one is respectable or unhappy over the whole
    earth.

So they show their relations to me and I accept them;
They bring me tokens of myself . . . . they evince
    them plainly in their possession.

I do not know where they got those tokens,
I must have passed that way untold times ago and
    negligently dropt them,
Myself moving forward then and now and forever,
Gathering and showing more always and with
    velocity,

Infinite and omnigenous and the like of these among
    them;
Not too exclusive toward the reachers of my
    remembrancers,
Picking out here one that I love,
Choosing to go with him on brotherly terms.

A gigantic beauty of a stallion, fresh and responsive
    to my caresses,
Head high in the forehead and wide between the
    ears,
Limbs glossy and supple, tail dusting the ground,
Eyes well apart and full of sparkling wickedness
    . . . . ears finely cut and flexibly moving.

His nostrils dilate . . . . my heels embrace him
    . . . . his well built limbs tremble with pleasure
    . . . . we speed around and return.

I but use you a moment and then I resign you stallion
    . . . . and do not need your paces, and outgallop
    them,
And myself as I stand or sit pass faster than you.

Swift wind! Space! My Soul! Now I know it is true
    what I guessed at;

What I guessed when I loafed on the grass,
What I guessed while I lay alone in my bed . . . . and
    again as I walked the beach under the paling stars
    of the morning.

My ties and ballasts leave me . . . . I travel . . . . I sail
    . . . . my elbows rest in the sea-gaps,
I skirt the sierras . . . . my palms cover continents,
I am afoot with my vision.

By the city's quadrangular houses . . . . in log-huts,
    or camping with lumbermen,
Along the ruts of the turnpike . . . . along the dry
    gulch and rivulet bed,
Hoeing my onion-patch, and rows of carrots and
    parsnips . . . . crossing savannas . . . . trailing in
    forests,
Prospecting . . . . gold-digging . . . . girdling the trees
    of a new purchase,
Scorched ankle-deep by the hot sand . . . . hauling
    my boat down the shallow river;
Where the panther walks to and fro on a limb
    overhead . . . . where the buck turns furiously at
    the hunter,
Where the rattlesnake suns his flabby length on a
    rock . . . . where the otter is feeding on fish,

Where the alligator in his tough pimples sleeps by
   the bayou,
Where the black bear is searching for roots or honey
   . . . . where the beaver pats the mud with his
   paddle-tail;
Over the growing sugar . . . . over the cottonplant
   . . . . over the rice in its low moist field;
Over the sharp-peaked farmhouse with its scalloped
   scum and slender shoots from the gutters;
Over the western persimmon . . . . over the
   longleaved corn and the delicate blueflowered flax;
Over the white and brown buckwheat, a hummer and
   a buzzer there with the rest,
Over the dusky green of the rye as it ripples and
   shades in the breeze;
Scaling mountains . . . . pulling myself cautiously up
   . . . . holding on by low scragged limbs,
Walking the path worn in the grass and beat through
   the leaves of the brush;
Where the quail is whistling betwixt the woods and
   the wheatlot,
Where the bat flies in the July eve . . . . where the
   great goldbug drops through the dark;
Where the flails keep time on the barn floor,
Where the brook puts out of the roots of the old
   tree and flows to the meadow,

Where cattle stand and shake away flies with the
    tremulous shuddering of their hides,
Where the cheese-cloth hangs in the kitchen, and
    andirons straddle the hearth-slab, and cobwebs fall
    in festoons from the rafters;
Where triphammers crash . . . . where the press is
    whirling its cylinders;
Wherever the human heart beats with terrible throes
    out of its ribs;
Where the pear-shaped balloon is floating aloft
    . . . . floating in it myself and looking composedly
    down;
Where the life-car is drawn on the slipnoose
    . . . . where the heat hatches pale-green eggs in the
    dented sand,
Where the she-whale swims with her calves and
    never forsakes them,
Where the steamship trails hindways its long
    pennant of smoke,
Where the ground-shark's fin cuts like a black chip
    out of the water,
Where the half-burned brig is riding on unknown
    currents,
Where shells grow to her slimy deck, and the dead
    are corrupting below;

Where the striped and starred flag is borne at the
  head of the regiments;
Approaching Manhattan, up by the long-stretching
  island,
Under Niagara, the cataract falling like a veil over
  my countenance;
Upon a door-step . . . . upon the horse-block of hard
  wood outside,
Upon the race-course, or enjoying picnics or jigs or
  a good game of baseball,
At he-festivals with blackguard jibes and ironical
  license and bull-dances and drinking and
  laughter,
At the cider-mill, tasting the sweet of the brown
  sqush . . . . sucking the juice through a straw,
At apple-peelings, wanting kisses for all the red fruit
  I find,
At musters and beach-parties and friendly bees and
  huskings and house-raisings;
Where the mockingbird sounds his delicious gurgles,
  and cackles and screams and weeps,
Where the hay-rick stands in the barnyard, and the
  dry-stalks are scattered, and the brood cow waits
  in the hovel,
Where the bull advances to do his masculine work,

and the stud to the mare, and the cock is treading
the hen,
Where the heifers browse, and the geese nip their
food with short jerks;
Where the sundown shadows lengthen over the
limitless and lonesome prairie,
Where the herds of buffalo make a crawling spread
of the square miles far and near;
Where the hummingbird shimmers . . . . where the
neck of the longlived swan is curving and winding;
Where the laughing-gull scoots by the slappy shore
and laughs her near-human laugh;
Where beehives range on a gray bench in the garden
half-hid by the high weeds;
Where the band-necked partridges roost in a ring on
the ground with their heads out;
Where burial coaches enter the arched gates of a
cemetery;
Where winter wolves bark amid wastes of snow and
icicled trees;
Where the yellow-crowned heron comes to the edge
of the marsh at night and feeds upon small crabs;
Where the splash of swimmers and divers cools the
warm noon;
Where the katydid works her chromatic reed on the
walnut-tree over the well;

Through patches of citrons and cucumbers with
    silver-wired leaves,
Through the salt-lick or orange glade . . . . or under
    conical firs;
Through the gymnasium . . . . through the curtained
    saloon . . . . through the office or public hall;
Pleased with the native and pleased with the foreign
    . . . . pleased with the new and old,
Pleased with women, the homely as well as the handsome,
Pleased with the quakeress as she puts off her bonnet
    and talks melodiously,
Pleased with the primitive tunes of the choir of the
    whitewashed church,
Pleased with the earnest words of the sweating
    Methodist preacher, or any preacher . . . . looking
    seriously at the camp-meeting;
Looking in at the shop-windows of Broadway the
    whole forenoon . . . . flatting the flesh of my nose
    on the thick plate-glass,
Wandering the same afternoon with my face turned
    up to the clouds;
My right and left arms round the sides of two friends
    and I in the middle;
Coming home with the bearded and dark-cheeked
    bush-boy . . . . riding behind him at the drape of
    the day;

Far from the settlements studying the print of
     animals' feet, or the moccasin print;
By the cot in the hospital reaching lemonade to a
     feverish patient,
By the coffined corpse when all is still, examining
     with a candle;
Voyaging to every port to dicker and adventure;
Hurrying with the modern crowd, as eager and fickle
     as any,
Hot toward one I hate, ready in my madness to knife
     him;
Solitary at midnight in my back yard, my thoughts
     gone from me a long while,
Walking the old hills of Judea with the beautiful
     gentle god by my side;
Speeding through space . . . . speeding through
     heaven and the stars,
Speeding amid the seen satellites and the broad ring
     and the diameter of eighty thousand miles,
Speeding with tailed meteors . . . . throwing fire-balls
     like the rest,
Carrying the crescent child that carries its own full
     mother in its belly;
Storming enjoying planning loving cautioning,
Backing and filling, appearing and disappearing,
I tread day and night such roads.

I visit the orchards of God and look at the spheric
    product,
And look at quintillions ripened, and look at
    quintillions green.

I fly the flight of the fluid and swallowing soul,
My course runs below the soundings of plummets.

I help myself to material and immaterial,
No guard can shut me off, no law can prevent me.

I anchor my ship for a little while only,
My messengers continually cruise away or bring their
    returns to me.

I go hunting polar furs and the seal . . . . leaping
    chasms with a pike-pointed staff . . . . clinging to
    topples of brittle and blue.

I ascend to the foretruck . . . . I take my place late at
    night in the crow's nest . . . . we sail through the
    arctic sea . . . . it is plenty light enough,
Through the clear atmosphere I stretch around on
    the wonderful beauty,
The enormous masses of ice pass me and I pass them
    . . . . the scenery is plain in all directions,

The white-topped mountains point up in the
    distance . . . . I fling out my fancies toward them;
We are approaching some great battlefield in which
    we are soon to be engaged,
We pass the colossal outposts of the encampments
    . . . . we pass with still feet and caution;
Or we are entering by the suburbs some vast and
    ruined city . . . . the blocks and fallen architecture
    more than all the living cities of the globe.

I am a free companion . . . . I bivouac by invading
    watchfires.

I turn the bridegroom out of bed and stay with the
    bride myself,
And tighten her all night to my thighs and lips.

My voice is the wife's voice, the screech by the rail
    of the stairs,
They fetch my man's body up dripping and
    drowned.

I understand the large hearts of heroes,
The courage of present times and all times;
How the skipper saw the crowded and rudderless

wreck of the steamship, and death chasing it up
  and down the storm,
How he knuckled tight and gave not back one inch,
  and was faithful of days and faithful of nights,
And chalked in large letters on a board, Be of good
  cheer, We will not desert you;
How he saved the drifting company at last,
How the lank loose-gowned women looked when
  boated from the side of their prepared graves,
How the silent old-faced infants, and the lifted sick,
  and the sharp-lipped unshaved men;
All this I swallow and it tastes good . . . . I like it
  well, it becomes mine,
I am the man . . . . I suffered . . . . I was there.

The disdain and calmness of martyrs,
The mother condemned for a witch and burnt with
  dry wood, and her children gazing on;
The hounded slave that flags in the race and leans by
  the fence, blowing and covered with sweat,
The twinges that sting like needles his legs and neck,
The murderous buckshot and the bullets,
All these I feel or am.

I am the hounded slave . . . . I wince at the bite of
  the dogs,

Hell and despair are upon me . . . . crack and again
     crack the marksmen,
I clutch the rails of the fence . . . . my gore dribs
     thinned with the ooze of my skin,
I fall on the weeds and stones,
The riders spur their unwilling horses and haul close,
They taunt my dizzy ears . . . . they beat me violently
     over the head with their whip-stocks.

Agonies are one of my changes of garments;
I do not ask the wounded person how he feels . . . .
     I myself become the wounded person,
My hurt turns livid upon me as I lean on a cane and
     observe.

I am the mashed fireman with breastbone broken
     . . . . tumbling walls buried me in their debris,
Heat and smoke I inspired . . . . I heard the yelling
     shouts of my comrades,
I heard the distant click of their picks and shovels;
They have cleared the beams away . . . . they tenderly
     lift me forth.

I lie in the night air in my red shirt . . . . the
     pervading hush is for my sake,
Painless after all I lie, exhausted but not so unhappy,

White and beautiful are the faces around me . . . .
  the heads are bared of their fire-caps,
The kneeling crowd fades with the light of the
  torches.

Distant and dead resuscitate,
They show as the dial or move as the hands of me
  . . . . and I am the clock myself.

I am an old artillerist, and tell of my fort's
  bombardment . . . . and am there again.

Again the reveille of drummers . . . . again the
  attacking cannon and mortars and howitzers,
Again the attacked send their cannon responsive.

I take part . . . . I see and hear the whole,
The cries and curses and roar . . . . the plaudits for
  well aimed shots,
The ambulanza slowly passing and trailing its red
  drip,
Workmen searching after damages, making
  indispensable repairs,
The fall of grenades through the rent roof . . . . the
  fan-shaped explosion,

The whizz of limbs heads stone wood and iron high
    in the air.

Again gurgles the mouth of my dying general . . . . he
    furiously waves with his hand,
He gasps through the clot . . . . Mind not me
    . . . . mind . . . . the entrenchments.

I tell not the fall of Alamo . . . . not one escaped to
    tell the fall of Alamo,
The hundred and fifty are dumb yet at Alamo.

Hear now the tale of a jetblack sunrise,
Hear of the murder in cold blood of four hundred
    and twelve young men.

Retreating they had formed in a hollow square with
    their baggage for breastworks,
Nine hundred lives out of the surrounding enemy's
    nine times their number was the price they took
    in advance,
Their colonel was wounded and their ammunition
    gone,
They treated for an honorable capitulation, received
    writing and seal, gave up their arms, and marched
    back prisoners of war.

They were the glory of the race of rangers,

Matchless with a horse, a rifle, a song, a supper or a
  courtship,

Large, turbulent, brave, handsome, generous, proud
  and affectionate,

Bearded, sunburnt, dressed in the free costume of
  hunters,

Not a single one over thirty years of age.

The second Sunday morning they were brought out
  in squads and massacred . . . . it was beautiful early
  summer,

The work commenced about five o'clock and was
  over by eight.

None obeyed the command to kneel,

Some made a mad and helpless rush . . . . some stood
  stark and straight,

A few fell at once, shot in the temple or heart
    . . . . the living and dead lay together,

The maimed and mangled dug in the dirt . . . . the
  new-comers saw them there;

Some half-killed attempted to crawl away,

These were dispatched with bayonets or battered
  with the blunts of muskets;

A youth not seventeen years old seized his assassin
    till two more came to release him,
The three were all torn, and covered with the boy's
    blood.

At eleven o'clock began the burning of the bodies;
And that is the tale of the murder of the four
    hundred and twelve young men,
And that was a jetblack sunrise.

Did you read in the seabooks of the oldfashioned
    frigate-fight?
Did you learn who won by the light of the moon
    and stars?

Our foe was no skulk in his ship, I tell you,
His was the English pluck, and there is no tougher
    or truer, and never was, and never will be;
Along the lowered eve he came, horribly raking us.

We closed with him . . . . the yards entangled . . . . the
    cannon touched,
My captain lashed fast with his own hands.

We had received some eighteen-pound shots under
    the water,

On our lower-gun-deck two large pieces had burst at the first fire, killing all around and blowing up overhead.

Ten o'clock at night, and the full moon shining and the leaks on the gain, and five feet of water reported,
The master-at-arms loosing the prisoners confined in the after-hold to give them a chance for themselves.

The transit to and from the magazine was now stopped by the sentinels,
They saw so many strange faces they did not know whom to trust.

Our frigate was afire . . . . the other asked if we demanded quarter? if our colors were struck and the fighting done?

I laughed content when I heard the voice of my little captain,
We have not struck, he composedly cried, We have just begun our part of the fighting.

Only three guns were in use,
One was directed by the captain himself against the enemy's mainmast,

Two well-served with grape and canister silenced his
    musketry and cleared his decks.

The tops alone seconded the fire of this little battery,
    especially the maintop,
They all held out bravely during the whole of the
    action.

Not a moment's cease,
The leaks gained fast on the pumps . . . . the fire eat
    toward the powder-magazine,
One of the pumps was shot away . . . . it was
    generally thought we were sinking.

Serene stood the little captain,
He was not hurried . . . . his voice was neither high
    nor low,
His eyes gave more light to us than our battle-
    lanterns.

Toward twelve at night, there in the beams of the
    moon they surrendered to us.

Stretched and still lay the midnight,
Two great hulls motionless on the breast of the
    darkness,

Our vessel riddled and slowly sinking
     . . . . preparations to pass to the one we had
     conquered,
The captain on the quarter deck coldly giving his
     orders through a countenance white as a sheet,
Near by the corpse of the child that served in the
     cabin,
The dead face of an old salt with long white hair
     and carefully curled whiskers,
The flames spite of all that could be done flickering
     aloft and below,
The husky voices of the two or three officers yet fit
     for duty,
Formless stacks of bodies and bodies by themselves
     . . . . dabs of flesh upon the masts and spars,
The cut of cordage and dangle of rigging . . . . the
     slight shock of the soothe of waves,
Black and impassive guns, and litter of powder-
     parcels, and the strong scent,
Delicate sniffs of the seabreeze . . . . smells of sedgy
     grass and fields by the shore . . . . death-messages
     given in charge to survivors,
The hiss of the surgeon's knife and the gnawing teeth
     of his saw,
The wheeze, the cluck, the swash of falling blood

. . . . the short wild scream, the long dull tapering
groan,
These so . . . . these irretrievable.

O Christ! My fit is mastering me!
What the rebel said gaily adjusting his throat to the
rope-noose,
What the savage at the stump, his eye-sockets empty,
his mouth spirting whoops and defiance,
What stills the traveler come to the vault at Mount
Vernon,
What sobers the Brooklyn boy as he looks down the
shores of the Wallabout and remembers the prison
ships,
What burnt the gums of the redcoat at Saratoga
when he surrendered his brigades,
These become mine and me every one, and they are
but little,
I become as much more as I like.

I embody all presences outlawed or suffering,
And see myself in prison shaped like another man,
And feel the dull unintermitted pain.

For me the keepers of convicts shoulder their
carbines and keep watch,
It is I let out in the morning and barred at night.

Not a mutineer walks handcuffed to the jail, but I
    am handcuffed to him and walk by his side,
I am less the jolly one there, and more the silent one
    with sweat on my twitching lips.

Not a youngster is taken for larceny, but I go up too
    and am tried and sentenced.

Not a cholera patient lies at the last gasp, but I also
    lie at the last gasp,
My face is ash-colored, my sinews gnarl . . . . away
    from me people retreat.

Askers embody themselves in me, and I am
    embodied in them,
I project my hat and sit shamefaced and beg.

I rise extatic through all, and sweep with the true
    gravitation,
The whirling and whirling is elemental within me.

Somehow I have been stunned. Stand back!
Give me a little time beyond my cuffed head and
    slumbers and dreams and gaping,
I discover myself on a verge of the usual mistake.

That I could forget the mockers and insults!
That I could forget the trickling tears and the blows
    of the bludgeons and hammers!
That I could look with a separate look on my own
    crucifixion and bloody crowning!

I remember . . . . I resume the overstaid fraction,
The grave of rock multiplies what has been confided
    to it . . . . or to any graves,
The corpses rise . . . . the gashes heal . . . . the
    fastenings roll away.

I troop forth replenished with supreme power, one
    of an average unending procession,
We walk the roads of Ohio and Massachusetts and
    Virginia and Wisconsin and New York and New
    Orleans and Texas and Montreal and San
    Francisco and Charleston and Savannah and
    Mexico,
Inland and by the seacoast and boundary lines
    . . . . and we pass the boundary lines.

Our swift ordinances are on their way over the whole
    earth,

The blossoms we wear in our hats are the growth of
  two thousand years.

Eleves I salute you,
I see the approach of your numberless gangs I
  see you understand yourselves and me,
And know that they who have eyes are divine, and
  the blind and lame are equally divine,
And that my steps drag behind yours yet go before
  them,
And are aware how I am with you no more than I
  am with everybody.

The friendly and flowing savage . . . . Who is he?
Is he waiting for civilization or past it and mastering
  it?

Is he some southwesterner raised outdoors? Is he
  Canadian?
Is he from the Mississippi country? or from Iowa,
  Oregon or California? or from the mountains? or
  prairie life or bush-life? or from the sea?

Wherever he goes men and women accept and desire
  him,

They desire he should like them and touch them and
  speak to them and stay with them.

Behaviour lawless as snow-flakes . . . . words simple
  as grass . . . . uncombed head and laughter and
  naiveté;
Slowstepping feet and the common features, and the
  common modes and emanations,
They descend in new forms from the tips of his
  fingers,
They are wafted with the odor of his body or breath
  . . . . they fly out of the glance of his eyes.

Flaunt of the sunshine I need not your bask . . . . lie
  over,
You light surfaces only . . . . I force the surfaces and
  the depths also.

Earth! you seem to look for something at my hands,
Say old topknot! what do you want?

Man or woman! I might tell how I like you, but
  cannot,
And might tell what it is in me and what it is in you,
  but cannot,

And might tell the pinings I have . . . . the pulse of
    my nights and days.

Behold I do not give lectures or a little charity,
What I give I give out of myself.

You there, impotent, loose in the knees, open your
    scarfed chops till I blow grit within you,
Spread your palms and lift the flaps of your pockets,
I am not to be denied . . . . I compel . . . . I have
    stores plenty and to spare,
And any thing I have I bestow.

I do not ask who you are . . . . that is not important
    to me,
You can do nothing and be nothing but what I will
    infold you.

To a drudge of the cottonfields or emptier of privies
    I lean . . . . on his right cheek I put the family kiss,
And in my soul I swear I never will deny him.

On women fit for conception I start bigger and
    nimbler babes,
This day I am jetting the stuff of far more arrogant
    republics.

To any one dying . . . . thither I speed and twist the
    knob of the door,
Turn the bedclothes toward the foot of the bed,
Let the physician and the priest go home.

I seize the descending man . . . . I raise him with
    resistless will.

O despairer, here is my neck,
By God! you shall not go down! Hang your whole
    weight upon me.

I dilate you with tremendous breath . . . . I buoy you
    up;
Every room of the house do I fill with an armed
    force . . . . lovers of me, bafflers of graves:
Sleep! I and they keep guard all night;
Not doubt, not decease shall dare to lay finger upon
    you,
I have embraced you, and henceforth possess you to
    myself,
And when you rise in the morning you will find what
    I tell you is so.

I am he bringing help for the sick as they pant on
    their backs,

And for strong upright men I bring yet more needed
   help.

I heard what was said of the universe,
Heard it and heard of several thousand years;
It is middling well as far as it goes . . . . but is that
   all?

Magnifying and applying come I,
Outbidding at the start the old cautious hucksters,
The most they offer for mankind and eternity less
   than a spirt of my own seminal wet,
Taking myself the exact dimensions of Jehovah and
   laying them away,
Lithographing Kronos and Zeus his son, and
   Hercules his grandson,
Buying drafts of Osiris and Isis and Belus and
   Brahma and Buddha,
In my portfolio placing Manito loose, and Allah on
   a leaf, and the crucifix engraved,
With Odin, and the hideous-faced Mexitli, and all
   idols and images,
Taking them all for what they are worth, and not a
   cent more,
Admitting they were alive and did the work of their
   day,

Admitting they bore mites as for unfledged birds
who have now to rise and fly and sing for
themselves,
Accepting the rough deific sketches to fill out better
in myself . . . . bestowing them freely on each man
and woman I see,
Discovering as much or more in a framer framing a
house,
Putting higher claims for him there with his rolled-
up sleeves, driving the mallet and chisel;
Not objecting to special revelations . . . . considering
a curl of smoke or a hair on the back of my hand
as curious as any revelation;
Those ahold of fire-engines and hook-and-ladder
ropes more to me than the gods of the antique
wars,
Minding their voices peal through the crash of
destruction,
Their brawny limbs passing safe over charred laths
. . . . their white foreheads whole and unhurt out
of the flames;
By the mechanic's wife with her babe at her nipple
interceding for every person born;
Three scythes at harvest whizzing in a row from
three lusty angels with shirts bagged out at their
waists;

The snag-toothed hostler with red hair redeeming
  sins past and to come,
Selling all he possesses and traveling on foot to fee
  lawyers for his brother and sit by him while he is
  tried for forgery:
What was strewn in the amplest strewing the square
  rod about me, and not filling the square rod then;
The bull and the bug never worshipped half enough,
Dung and dirt more admirable than was dreamed,
The supernatural of no account . . . . myself waiting
  my time to be one of the supremes,
The day getting ready for me when I shall do as
  much good as the best, and be as prodigious,
Guessing when I am it will not tickle me much to
  receive puffs out of pulpit or print;
By my life-lumps! becoming already a creator!
Putting myself here and now to the ambushed womb
  of the shadows!

. . . . A call in the midst of the crowd,
My own voice, orotund sweeping and final.

Come my children,
Come my boys and girls, and my women and
  household and intimates,

Now the performer launches his nerve . . . . he has
   passed his prelude on the reeds within.

Easily written loosefingered chords! I feel the thrum
   of their climax and close.

My head slues round on my neck,
Music rolls, but not from the organ . . . . folks are
   around me, but they are no household of mine.

Ever the hard and unsunk ground,
Ever the eaters and drinkers . . . . ever the upward
   and downward sun . . . . ever the air and the
   ceaseless tides,
Ever myself and my neighbors, refreshing and wicked
   and real,
Ever the old inexplicable query . . . . ever that
   thorned thumb—that breath of itches and thirsts,
Ever the vexer's hoot! hoot! till we find where the sly
   one hides and bring him forth;
Ever love . . . . ever the sobbing liquid of life,
Ever the bandage under the chin . . . . ever the tressels
   of death.

Here and there with dimes on the eyes walking,
To feed the greed of the belly the brains liberally
   spooning,

Tickets buying or taking or selling, but in to the
   feast never once going;
Many sweating and ploughing and thrashing, and
   then the chaff for payment receiving,
A few idly owning, and they the wheat continually
   claiming.

This is the city . . . . and I am one of the citizens;
Whatever interests the rest interests me . . . . politics,
   churches, newspapers, schools,
Benevolent societies, improvements, banks, tariffs,
   steamships, factories, markets,
Stocks and stores and real estate and personal estate.

The little plentiful manikins skipping around in
   collars and tailed coats . . . . I am aware who they
   are . . . . and that they are not worms or fleas,
I acknowledge the duplicates of myself under all the
   scrape-lipped and pipe-legged concealments.

The weakest and shallowest is deathless with me,
What I do and say the same waits for them,
Every thought that flounders in me the same
   flounders in them.

I know perfectly well my own egotism,
And know my omniverous words, and cannot say
   any less,

And would fetch you whoever you are flush with
    myself.

My words are words of a questioning, and to
    indicate reality;
This printed and bound book . . . . but the printer
    and the printing-office boy?
The marriage estate and settlement . . . . but the body
    and mind of the bridegroom? also those of the
    bride?
The panorama of the sea . . . . but the sea itself?
The well-taken photographs . . . . but your wife or
    friend close and solid in your arms?
The fleet of ships of the line and all the modern
    improvements . . . . but the craft and pluck of the
    admiral?
The dishes and fare and furniture . . . . but the host
    and hostess, and the look out of their eyes?
The sky up there . . . . yet here or next door or across
    the way?
The saints and sages in history . . . . but you yourself?
Sermons and creeds and theology . . . . but the human
    brain, and what is called reason, and what is called
    love, and what is called life?

I do not despise you priests;
My faith is the greatest of faiths and the least of
    faiths,

Enclosing all worship ancient and modern, and all
  between ancient and modern,
Believing I shall come again upon the earth after five
  thousand years,
Waiting responses from oracles . . . . honoring the
  gods . . . . saluting the sun,
Making a fetish of the first rock or stump
  . . . . powowing with sticks in the circle of
  obis,
Helping the lama or brahmin as he trims the lamps
  of the idols,
Dancing yet through the streets in a phallic
  procession . . . . rapt and austere in the woods, a
  gymnosophist,
Drinking mead from the skull-cup . . . . to shasta and
  vedas admirant . . . . minding the koran,
Walking the teokallis, spotted with gore from the
  stone and knife—beating the serpent-skin drum;
Accepting the gospels, accepting him that was
  crucified, knowing assuredly that he is divine,
To the mass kneeling—to the puritan's prayer
  rising—sitting patiently in a pew,
Ranting and frothing in my insane crisis—waiting
  dead-like till my spirit arouses me;
Looking forth on pavement and land, and outside of
  pavement and land,
Belonging to the winders of the circuit of circuits.

One of that centripetal and centrifugal gang,
I turn and talk like a man leaving charges before a
    journey.

Down-hearted doubters, dull and excluded,
Frivolous sullen moping angry affected disheartened
    atheistical,
I know every one of you, I know the sea of torment,
    despair and unbelief.

How the flukes splash!
How they contort rapid as lightning, with spasms
    and spouts of blood!

Be at peace bloody flukes of doubters and sullen
    mopers,
I take my place among you as much as among any;
The past is the push of you and me and all precisely
    the same,
And the night is for you and me and all,
And what is yet untried and afterward is for you and
    me and all.

I do not know what is untried and afterward,
But I know it is sure and alive and sufficient.

Each who passes is considered, and each who stops
    is considered, and not a single one can it fail.

It cannot fail the young man who died and was
    buried,
Nor the young woman who died and was put by his
    side,
Nor the little child that peeped in at the door and
    then drew back and was never seen again,
Nor the old man who has lived without purpose, and
    feels it with bitterness worse than gall,
Nor him in the poorhouse tubercled by rum and the
    bad disorder,
Nor the numberless slaughtered and wrecked
    . . . . nor the brutish koboo, called the ordure of
    humanity,
Nor the sacs merely floating with open mouths for
    food to slip in,
Nor any thing in the earth, or down in the oldest
    graves of the earth,
Nor any thing in the myriads of spheres, nor one of
    the myriads of myriads that inhabit them,
Nor the present, nor the least wisp that is known.

It is time to explain myself . . . . let us stand up.

What is known I strip away . . . . I launch all men
    and women forward with me into the unknown.

The clock indicates the moment . . . . but what does
    eternity indicate?

Eternity lies in bottomless reservoirs . . . . its buckets
    are rising forever and ever,
They pour and they pour and they exhale away.

We have thus far exhausted trillions of winters and
    summers;
There are trillions ahead, and trillions ahead of them.

Births have brought us richness and variety,
And other births will bring us richness and variety.

I do not call one greater and one smaller,
That which fills its period and place is equal to any.

Were mankind murderous or jealous upon you my
    brother or my sister?
I am sorry for you . . . . they are not murderous or
    jealous upon me;
All has been gentle with me . . . . . . I keep no account
    with lamentation;
What have I to do with lamentation?

I am an acme of things accomplished, and I an
    encloser of things to be.

My feet strike an apex of the apices of the stairs,
On every step bunches of ages, and larger bunches
    between the steps,
All below duly traveled—and still I mount and
    mount.

Rise after rise bow the phantoms behind me,
Afar down I see the huge first Nothing, the vapor
    from the nostrils of death,
I know I was even there . . . . I waited unseen and
    always,
And slept while God carried me through the
    lethargic mist,
And took my time . . . . and took no hurt from the
    fetid carbon.

Long I was hugged close . . . . long and long.

Immense have been the preparations for me,
Faithful and friendly the arms that have helped me.

Cycles ferried my cradle, rowing and rowing like
    cheerful boatmen;
For room to me stars kept aside in their own rings,
They sent influences to look after what was to hold
    me.

Before I was born out of my mother generations
  guided me,
My embryo has never been torpid . . . . nothing could
  overlay it;
For it the nebula cohered to an orb . . . . the long
  slow strata piled to rest it on . . . . vast vegetables
  gave it sustenance,
Monstrous sauroids transported it in their mouths
  and deposited it with care.

All forces have been steadily employed to complete
  and delight me,
Now I stand on this spot with my soul.

Span of youth! Ever-pushed elasticity! Manhood
  balanced and florid and full!

My lovers suffocate me!
Crowding my lips, and thick in the pores of my skin,
Jostling me through streets and public halls
  . . . . coming naked to me at night,
Crying by day Ahoy from the rocks of the river
  . . . . swinging and chirping over my head,
Calling my name from flowerbeds or vines or tangled
  underbrush,
Or while I swim in the bath . . . . or drink from the

pump at the corner . . . . or the curtain is down at
    the opera . . . . or I glimpse at a woman's face in
    the railroad car;
Lighting on every moment of my life,
Bussing my body with soft and balsamic busses,
Noiselessly passing handfuls out of their hearts and
    giving them to be mine.

Old age superbly rising! Ineffable grace of dying
    days!

Every condition promulges not only itself . . . . it
    promulges what grows after and out of itself,
And the dark hush promulges as much as any.

I open my scuttle at night and see the far-sprinkled
    systems,
And all I see, multiplied as high as I can cipher, edge
    but the rim of the farther systems.

Wider and wider they spread, expanding and always
    expanding,
Outward and outward and forever outward.

My sun has his sun, and round him obediently
    wheels,

He joins with his partners a group of superior circuit,
And greater sets follow, making specks of the
greatest inside them.

There is no stoppage, and never can be stoppage;
If I and you and the worlds and all beneath or upon
their surfaces, and all the palpable life, were this
moment reduced back to a pallid float, it would
not avail in the long run,
We should surely bring up again where we now
stand,
And as surely go as much farther, and then farther
and farther.

A few quadrillions of eras, a few octillions of cubic
leagues, do not hazard the span, or make it
impatient,
They are but parts . . . . any thing is but a part.

See ever so far . . . . there is limitless space outside
of that,
Count ever so much . . . . there is limitless time
around that.

Our rendezvous is fitly appointed . . . . God will be
there and wait till we come.

I know I have the best of time and space—and that
    I was never measured, and never will be measured.

I tramp a perpetual journey,
My signs are a rain-proof coat and good shoes and a
    staff cut from the woods;
No friend of mine takes his ease in my chair,
I have no chair, nor church nor philosophy;
I lead no man to a dinner-table or library or
    exchange,
But each man and each woman of you I lead upon a
    knoll,
My left hand hooks you round the waist,
My right hand points to landscapes of continents,
    and a plain public road.

Not I, not any one else can travel that road for you,
You must travel it for yourself.

It is not far . . . . it is within reach,
Perhaps you have been on it since you were born,
    and did not know,
Perhaps it is every where on water and on land.

Shoulder your duds, and I will mine, and let us
    hasten forth;

Wonderful cities and free nations we shall fetch as
   we go.

If you tire, give me both burdens, and rest the chuff
   of your hand on my hip,
And in due time you shall repay the same service to
   me;
For after we start we never lie by again.

This day before dawn I ascended a hill and looked
   at the crowded heaven,
And I said to my spirit, When we become the
   enfolders of those orbs and the pleasure and
   knowledge of every thing in them, shall we be
   filled and satisfied then?
And my spirit said No, we level that lift to pass and
   continue beyond.

You are also asking me questions, and I hear you;
I answer that I cannot answer . . . . you must find
   out for yourself.

Sit awhile wayfarer,
Here are biscuits to eat and here is milk to drink,
But as soon as you sleep and renew yourself in sweet

clothes I will certainly kiss you with my goodbye
kiss and open the gate for your egress hence.

Long enough have you dreamed contemptible
dreams,
Now I wash the gum from your eyes,
You must habit yourself to the dazzle of the light
and of every moment of your life.

Long have you timidly waded, holding a plank by
the shore,
Now I will you to be a bold swimmer,
To jump off in the midst of the sea, and rise again
and nod to me and shout, and laughingly dash
with your hair.

I am the teacher of athletes,
He that by me spreads a wider breast than my own
proves the width of my own,
He most honors my style who learns under it to
destroy the teacher.

The boy I love, the same becomes a man not through
derived power but in his own right,
Wicked, rather than virtuous out of conformity or
fear,

Fond of his sweetheart, relishing well his steak,
Unrequited love or a slight cutting him worse than a
    wound cuts,
First rate to ride, to fight, to hit the bull's eye, to sail
    a skiff, to sing a song or play on the banjo,
Preferring scars and faces pitted with smallpox over
    all latherers and those that keep out of the sun.

I teach straying from me, yet who can stray from me?
I follow you whoever you are from the present hour;
My words itch at your ears till you understand them.

I do not say these things for a dollar, or to fill up
    the time while I wait for a boat;
It is you talking just as much as myself . . . . I act as
    the tongue of you,
It was tied in your mouth . . . . in mine it begins to
    be loosened.

I swear I will never mention love or death inside a
    house,
And I swear I never will translate myself at all, only
    to him or her who privately stays with me in the
    open air.

If you would understand me go to the heights or
    water-shore,
The nearest gnat is an explanation and a drop or the
    motion of waves a key,
The maul the oar and the handsaw second my words.

No shuttered room or school can commune with me,
But roughs and little children better than they.

The young mechanic is closest to me . . . . he knows
    me pretty well,
The woodman that takes his axe and jug with him
    shall take me with him all day,
The farmboy ploughing in the field feels good at the
    sound of my voice,
In vessels that sail my words sail . . . . I go with
    fishermen and seamen, and love them,
My face rubs to the hunter's face when he lies down
    alone in his blanket,
The driver thinking of me does not mind the jolt of
    his wagon,
The young mother and old mother comprehend me,
The girl and the wife rest the needle a moment and
    forget where they are,
They and all would resume what I have told them.

I have said that the soul is not more than the body,
And I have said that the body is not more than the
    soul,
And nothing, not God, is greater to one than one's-
    self is,
And whoever walks a furlong without sympathy
    walks to his own funeral, dressed in his shroud,
And I or you pocketless of a dime may purchase the
    pick of the earth,
And to glance with an eye or show a bean in its pod
    confounds the learning of all times,
And there is no trade or employment but the young
    man following it may become a hero,
And there is no object so soft but it makes a hub for
    the wheeled universe,
And any man or woman shall stand cool and
    supercilious before a million universes.

And I call to mankind, Be not curious about God,
For I who am curious about each am not curious
    about God,
No array of terms can say how much I am at peace
    about God and about death.

I hear and behold God in every object, yet I
    understand God not in the least,

Nor do I understand who there can be more
wonderful than myself.

Why should I wish to see God better than this day?
I see something of God each hour of the twenty-
four, and each moment then,
In the faces of men and women I see God, and in
my own face in the glass;
I find letters from God dropped in the street, and
every one is signed by God's name,
And I leave them where they are, for I know that
others will punctually come forever and ever.

And as to you death, and you bitter hug of mortality
. . . . it is idle to try to alarm me.

To his work without flinching the accoucheur comes,
I see the elderhand pressing receiving supporting,
I recline by the sills of the exquisite flexible doors
. . . . and mark the outlet, and mark the relief and
escape.

And as to you corpse I think you are good manure,
but that does not offend me,
I smell the white roses sweetscented and growing,

I reach to the leafy lips .... I reach to the polished
   breasts of melons.

And as to you life, I reckon you are the leavings of
   many deaths,
No doubt I have died myself ten thousand times
   before.

I hear you whispering there O stars of heaven,
O suns .... O grass of graves .... O perpetual
   transfers and promotions .... if you do not say
   anything how can I say anything?

Of the turbid pool that lies in the autumn forest,
Of the moon that descends the steeps of the
   soughing twilight,
Toss, sparkles of day and dusk .... toss on the black
   stems that decay in the muck,
Toss to the moaning gibberish of the dry limbs.

I ascend from the moon .... I ascend from the
   night,
And perceive of the ghastly glitter the sunbeams
   reflected,
And debouch to the steady and central from the
   offspring great or small.

There is that in me . . . . I do not know what it is
    . . . . but I know it is in me.

Wrenched and sweaty . . . . calm and cool then my
    body becomes;
I sleep . . . . I sleep long.

I do not know it . . . . it is without name . . . . it is a
    word unsaid,
It is not in any dictionary or utterance or symbol.

Something it swings on more than the earth I swing
    on,
To it the creation is the friend whose embracing
    awakes me.

Perhaps I might tell more . . . . Outlines! I plead for
    my brothers and sisters.

Do you see O my brothers and sisters?
It is not chaos or death . . . . it is form and union
    and plan . . . . it is eternal life . . . . it is happiness.

The past and present wilt . . . . I have filled them and
    emptied them,
And proceed to fill my next fold of the future.

Listener up there! . . . . what have you to confide to
  me?
Look in my face while I snuff the sidle of evening,
Talk honestly, for no one else hears you, and I stay
  only a minute longer.

Do I contradict myself?
Very well then . . . . I contradict myself;
I am large . . . . I contain multitudes.

I concentrate toward them that are nigh . . . . I wait
  on the door-slab.

Who has done his day's work and will soonest be
  through with his supper?
Who wishes to walk with me?

Will you speak before I am gone? Will you prove
  already too late?

The spotted hawk swoops by and accuses me . . . . he
  complains of my gab and my loitering.

I too am not a bit tamed . . . . I too am
  untranslatable,

I sound my barbaric yawp over the roofs of the
world.

The last scud of day holds back for me,
It flings my likeness after the rest and true as any on
the shadowed wilds,
It coaxes me to the vapor and the dusk.

I depart as air . . . . I shake my white locks at the
runaway sun,
I effuse my flesh in eddies and drift it in lacy jags.

I bequeath myself to the dirt to grow from the grass
I love,
If you want me again look for me under your
bootsoles.

You will hardly know who I am or what I mean,
But I shall be good health to you nevertheless,
And filter and fibre your blood.

Failing to fetch me at first keep encouraged,
Missing me one place search another,
I stop some where waiting for you

Editor's Notes

General Note

Malcolm Cowley's *Leaves of Grass: The First (1855) Edition*, published in 1959, alerted contemporary readers to the original text of "Song of Myself." His introductory essay contains some insightful pages on the revisions, as does Galway Kinnell's introduction to *The Essential Whitman*. (Mr. Kinnell's book is apparently the first to present a conflated text of "Song of Myself"; I wasn't aware of it until I had completed work on mine.)

I would also like to recommend two excellent essays: "Some Lines from Whitman" in *Poetry and the Age* by Randall Jarrell and "A Draft of Whitman" in *The Gift: Imagination and the Erotic Life of Property* by Lewis Hyde.

Textual Notes

The first entry in each note is the revision I have adopted and the date of the edition it comes from (that edition's punctuation, if it differs from the 1855 norm, is indicated within brackets); the second entry is the text of the first edition.

p. xiii, l. 1—Song of Myself: 1876
  1855: no title

p. 4, l. 4—increase, always sex,: 1856
  1855: increase,/

p. 7, ll. 19f.—peace and knowledge: 1867
  1855: peace and joy and knowledge

p. 7, l. 20—all the argument: 1867
  1855: all the art and argument

p. 9, l. 14—old people, or: 1876
  1855: old people and from women, and

p. 12, ll. 13f.—I witness the corpse with its dabbled hair, I note where the pistol has fallen: 1867 [hair—I].
  1855: It is so . . . . I witnessed the corpse . . . . there the pistol had fallen.

p. 13, ll. 22f.—I come and I depart.: 1856
  1855: I come again and again.

p. 14, l. 18—Falling: 1867
  1855: Soundly falling

p. 15, ll. 15f.—neck . . . . he held his bride by the hand,: 1867 [neck—he held his bride by the hand;]
  1855: neck, / One hand rested on his rifle . . . . the other hand held firmly the wrist of the red girl,

p. 16, l. 2—limpsy: 1856
  1855: limpsey

p. 21, l. 22—Thanksgiving: 1860
1855: thanksgiving

p. 22, l. 24—auction-stand: 1871
1855: stand

p. 24, ll. 25f.—his first professions,: 1860
1855: the first professions,

p. 27, l. 1—adobe: 1856
1855: abode

p. 29, l. 22—behavior: 1860
1855: behaviour

p. 33, l. 1—Why should I pray? Why should: 1860
1855: Shall I pray? Shall

p. 33, ll. 3ff.—Having pried through the strata and ana-lyzed to a hair, and counselled with doctors and calcu-lated close,: 1860 [Having pried through the strata, analyzed to a hair, counsel'd with doctors and calcu-lated close,]

1855: I have pried through the strata and analyzed to a hair,

p. 33, l. 6—I find no sweeter fat than sticks to my own bones.: 1860

1855: And counselled with doctors and calculated close, and found no sweeter fat than sticks to my own bones.

p. 35, l. 8—development: 1856
1855: developement

p. 39, l. 12—imbuing: 1860
   1855: imbueing

p. 42, ll. 9f.—one thing more than another it shall be the spread of my own body, or any part of it;: 1867 [one thing more than another, it shall be the spread of my own body, or any part of it.]
   1855: any particular thing it shall be some of the spread of my body;

p. 47, l. 22—violoncello: 1860
   1855: violincello

p. 47, ll. 23ff.—I hear the keyed cornet, it glides quickly in through my ears, it shakes mad-sweet pangs through my belly and breast.: 1856
   1855: And hear the keyed cornet or else the echo of sunset.

p. 48, ll. 9f.—It wrenches such ardors from me, I did not know I possessed them,: 1856
   1855: It wrenches unnamable ardors from my breast,

p. 48, l. 16—throttled in fakes: 1860
   1855: squeezed in the fakes

p. 48, l. 17—At length let: 1860
   1855: Let

p. 52, l. 15—chef-d'œuvre: 1860
   1855: chef-d'ouvre

p. 52, l. 23—infidels.: 1860
   1855: infidels, / And I could come every afternoon

of my life to look at the farmer's girl boiling her iron tea kettle and baking shortcake.

p. 53, l. 11—mastodon: 1860
  1855: mastadon

p. 54, l. 3—long and long.: 1867
  1855: sometimes half the day long.

p. 54, l. 13—unhappy: 1876
  1855: industrious

p. 55, l. 5—one that I love,: 1856
  1855: one that shall be my amie,

p. 59, l. 16—apple-peelings: 1856
  1855: apple-pealings

p. 61, l. 17—of Broadway: 1860
  1855: in Broadway

p. 61, l. 18—flatting the flesh of my nose on: 1860
  1855: pressing the flesh of my nose to

p. 64, l. 3—We are approaching: 1856
  1855: We are about approaching

p. 65, l. 13—well, it: 1856 [well—it]
  1855: well and it

p. 67, l. 8—my fort's: 1856
  1855: some fort's

p. 67, ll. 18f.—damages, making indispensable: 1856
  1855: damages and to make indispensible

p. 71, l. 15—quarter?: 1856
   1855: quarters?

p. 74, l. 19—I embody all presences outlawed or suffering,: 1867 [outlaw'd or suffering;]
   1855: I become any presence or truth of humanity here,

p. 78, l. 5—naïveté;: 1860 [naïveté]
   1855: naivete;

p. 81, l. 16—Buddha,: 1856
   1855: Adonai,

p. 81, l. 21—Taking: 1856
   1855: Honestly taking

p. 84, l. 5—slues round: 1856
   1855: evolves

p. 85, l. 13—The little plentiful manikins skipping around: 1867
   1855: They who piddle and patter here

p. 88, ll. 7f.—you, I know the sea of torment, despair and unbelief.: 1867 [you—I]
   1855: you, and know the unspoken interrogatories, / By experience I know them.

p. 91, l. 14—fetid: 1860
   1855: foetid

p. 97, l. 7—life.: 1856
   1855: life

p. 99, l. 14—my words sail: 1856
  1855: my words must sail

p. 99, l. 20—old mother comprehend: 1856
  1855: old mother shall comprehend

p. 104, l. 1—there! . . . . what: 1881 [there! what]
  1855: there! Here you . . . . what